SURVIVOR

Scott O'Grady
Behind Enemy Lines

Barbara A. Somervill

HIGH
interest
books

Children's Press®
A Division of Scholastic Inc.
New York / Toronto / London / Auckland / Sydney
Mexico City / New Delhi / Hong Kong
Danbury, Connecticut

Book Design: Christopher Logan and Daniel Hosek
Contributing Editor: Matthew Pitt

Photo Credits: Cover, pp. 14, 16, 29, 39 © AP/Wide World Photos;
back cover, pp. 1, 5, 9, 17, 27, 37 courtesy of Defense Visual
Information Center, March ARB, California; p. 4 © Staff Sgt. John
C. Lasky/U.S. Air Force; p. 7 Daniel Hosek; p. 8 © Bettmann/
Corbis; p. 11 © Bohemian Nomad Picturemakers/Corbis; p. 12
© Terry Ashe/TimePix; p. 21 Tech Sgt. Michael Rivera/U.S. Air
Force; pp. 23, 26 © EPA/AFP; p. 24 Kyran V. Adams/U.S. Army;
p. 31 © Corbis; p. 36 © Peter Turnley/Corbis; pp. 42, 43, 44, 45,
46, 47, 48 © Photodisc

Library of Congress Cataloging-in-Publication Data

Somervill, Barbara A.
  Scott O'Grady : behind enemy lines / Barbara A. Somervill.
  p. cm. —(High interest books) (Survivor)
  Includes bibliographical references and index.
  ISBN 0-516-24332-2 (lib. bdg.) — ISBN 0-516-27871-1 (pbk.)
  1. O'Grady, Scott. 2. Yugoslav War, 1991-1995—Aerial
operations, American. 3. Yugoslav War, 1991-1995—Bosnia
and Herzegovina. 4. Yugoslav War, 1991-1995—Personal
narratives, American. 5. Fighter pilots—United States—
Biography. I. Title. II. Series. III. Series: Survivor

DR1313.7.A47S66 2003
949.703—dc21

                                    2002155013

Contents

Introduction

The missile didn't just graze Scott O'Grady's F-16 aircraft. It ripped his jet right in two.

It happened in June 1995. Midway through a peacekeeping mission over a war-torn section of Europe, O'Grady's life flashed before his eyes. An enemy missile rammed into his jet. The back half of the F-16 dropped away. The jet fuel burst into flames. Fire curled under his helmet.

There was barely any time to think. Quickly, O'Grady decided to eject from his cockpit. He grabbed and pulled a handle near the control panel. The jet canopy broke away. As O'Grady shot into the air and his parachute opened, his wrecked F-16 fell toward the ground.

Minutes later, O'Grady landed safely on the ground. However, there was nothing safe about

To keep the peace over Bosnian airspace, Captain O'Grady flew an F-16 like this one. This aircraft is one of the United States' most important air combat weapons.

the ground on which he landed. He was in enemy territory, behind enemy lines. In the skies, his F-16 provided him with speed and protection. Here, on the ground, he was a slow-moving target. Worst of all, he was alone. The battery that powered his radio was low. He wasn't even sure if his fellow soldiers could pick up his signals for help. He hoped those soldiers were looking for him. However, he couldn't stand in one place waiting for the rescue party. There were enemies hunting him, closing in with every hour. Scott O'Grady had cheated death when he ejected from his F-16. His race for survival, though, had just begun.

1 Site from which Captain Scott O'Grady launched his F-16 on June 2, 1995
2 Site where O'Grady's F-16 was blown apart by an enemy missile
3 Location where O'Grady landed following his emergency ejection
4 Area of enemy territory where O'Grady hid, trying to avoid capture
5 Site where O'Grady was rescued on June 8

▶

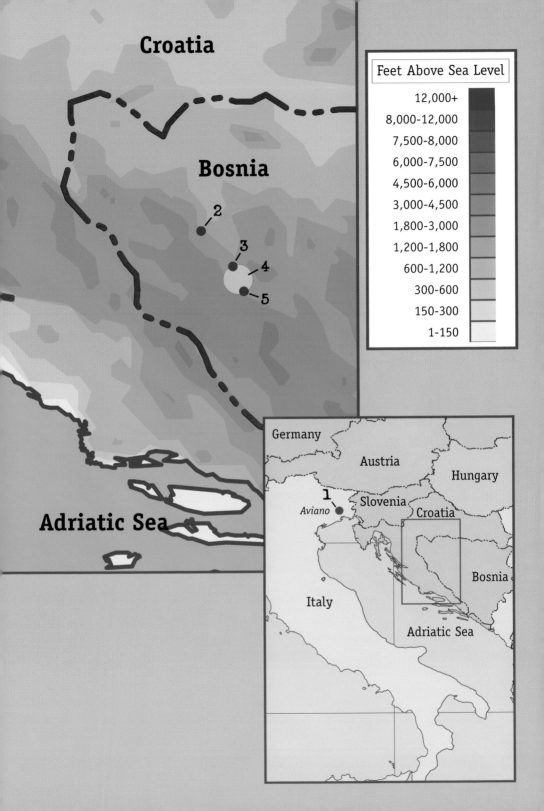

Croatia

Bosnia

2

3

4

5

Feet Above Sea Level

12,000+
8,000-12,000
7,500-8,000
6,000-7,500
4,500-6,000
3,000-4,500
1,800-3,000
1,200-1,800
600-1,200
300-600
150-300
1-150

Adriatic Sea

Germany

Austria

Hungary

1

Slovenia

Aviano

Croatia

Italy

Bosnia

Adriatic Sea

Scott's desire to take to the skies began at an early age. Once he got the urge to be a pilot, it never went away. This Cessna 150 is similar to the aircraft in which O'Grady first flew.

A Dream Takes Flight

Scott F. O'Grady was born in Brooklyn, New York, on October 12, 1965. He was the eldest of Mary and William O'Grady's three children. Scott's dad was a doctor in the United States Marines. William was assigned to different military bases, so the family moved many times.

Scott took his first plane ride when he was only six years old. At the time, his family was living in Long Beach, California. His father took him on a 70-minute trip in a Cessna 150. Scott's face lit up with joy. From that day on, Scott's dreams were all about flying.

Dark Cloud

By the time O'Grady turned nine, his family had settled in Spokane, Washington. After high school, he planned to go to the U.S. Air Force Academy, in Colorado Springs, Colorado. Although O'Grady's grades were strong, the academy did not accept him. His entrance exam scores were too low. The disappointment hurt O'Grady deeply. Still, he didn't give up. He wanted to fly, and he would succeed. He just needed to follow a different path.

A New Flight Path

O'Grady attended Embry-Riddle Aeronautical University, in Prescott, Arizona. At Embry-Riddle, he had plenty of flying practice. He also joined the Reserved Officer Training Corps (ROTC). The ROTC is a program run by the U.S. Army to train army officers. The ROTC gave O'Grady his first military service. During the summer of his sophomore year in college, O'Grady spent four weeks in field training. This training included a tough, two-day survival course. During the course, O'Grady learned that eating ants was a way to get needed protein. He was skeptical. "I decided I'd rather go hungry," he recalled thinking at the time.

The ROTC pushes its officers to their physical limits. O'Grady's ROTC training would come in handy during his stay in enemy territory.

O'Grady's education and confidence took off. The U.S. Air Force even paid for his last two years of college. After earning a degree in 1989, he joined the air force. For one year, he served in the North Atlantic Treaty Organization (NATO). NATO is an organization that protects the freedom and security of its nineteen member countries. O'Grady was part of a Joint Jet Pilot Training Program. It was located at Sheppard Air Force Base in Texas.

Only pilots as skilled and trusted as
O'Grady were allowed to ride inside the
U.S. Air Force's most costly fighter jets.

After Sheppard, O'Grady trained to fly F-16s
at Luke Air Force Base in Arizona. Nearly 50 feet
(15 meters) long and 16 feet (4.8 m) high, the
F-16 is a one-person, single-engine fighting jet.
F-16s are used to attack airfields, bomb military
facilities, and fight air-to-air dogfights. They can
reach speeds of 1,500 miles per hour (about
2,400 kilometers per hour). This speed, which is
nearly twice the speed of sound, is known as
Mach 2. F-16s carry a 20mm multi-barrel cannon
with five hundred rounds of ammunition. They
also carry up to six air-to-air missiles used for
shooting down enemy planes.

The air force pays about $19 million for each F-16. They trust only their finest pilots to fly these costly jets. Scott O'Grady was one of those pilots. O'Grady joined the 555th Fighter Squadron of the Thirty-first Fighter Wing. This squadron was nicknamed the "Triple Nickel." The 555th was stationed in the friendly territory of Aviano, Italy. However, they were flying their missions over much more hostile territory.

Operation Deny Flight

O'Grady was part of a United Nations (UN) peace-keeping mission in Bosnia. Bosnia is part of the Balkans, a group of nations in the southern part of Europe. At this time, a deadly civil war was being fought in Bosnia. Three ethnic groups— the Serbs, Muslims, and Croatians—were fighting with one another. An ethnic group is a group of people of the same race, religion, or culture. The UN mission was code named "Operation Deny Flight." NATO supplied flight crews from several

Fighting between ethnic groups in Bosnia forced families like this one to be separated. NATO and UN Forces helped ease the conflict.

countries. These fighter squadrons patrolled the skies above Bosnia.

The mission's goal was to prevent the three ethnic groups—the Serbs, Muslims, and Croatians—from flying in the no-fly zone. This was an area of Bosnian skies that was off-limits to the ethnic groups' aircraft. If any group disobeyed the order, the F-16 pilots would shoot them down. By enforcing the no-fly zone, the UN hoped to stop the bloodshed caused by the civil war.

The ethnic groups were angry that the NATO fighter squadrons were there. In fact, the Serbs had just captured 350 unarmed NATO military observers. O'Grady knew how dangerous the situation was. If he came into contact with anyone in Bosnia, he might become the next hostage.

Did You Know?

UN peacekeeping missions also help arrange fair elections and protect human rights.

After their jets came under enemy fire, Captain Bob "Wilbur" Wright (right) wasn't sure whether his friend Scott O'Grady (left) had survived the assault.

Two

"Missiles in the Air!"

June 2, 1995—Aviano, Italy

Today's mission would be Captain O'Grady's forty-seventh over Bosnia. It was a standard two-ship flight. O'Grady's good friend, Captain Bob "Wilbur" Wright, flew his jet in the lead position. O'Grady flew as wingman, behind Wright. The F-16s were scheduled to take off at 1315 hours (1:15 P.M.).

Lucky Look

As he was dressing for his mission, an article posted on a wall caught O'Grady's attention. The article was called "The Will to Survive." The article told the stories of two men involved in terrible accidents. One of the men was lost in the desert. For eight days, he went without a drop of water. He should have died of dehydration, but

Did You Know?

The military uses a 24-hour clock to tell time. That way, there is no confusion between morning and evening hours. This means that 0830 hours is 8:30 A.M. However, 8:30 P.M. is 2030 hours.

his will to survive carried him through until his rescue. The second story followed a pilot whose small plane crashed in Alaska. The man signaled for help using his radio. Nevertheless, he grew discouraged. He was sure no one had heard his call— so he took his own life. Tragically, rescue helicopters found his body just one day later. They had heard his cry for help. The stories moved O'Grady, making him see how important it was to assume the best, even in bad conditions.

O'Grady ate a few slices of pizza for lunch. He didn't know this would be his last full meal for nearly a week. Wright and O'Grady discussed what they would do if either man were shot down. Then they checked their gear. Each pilot wore a gravity suit. This protected them from the pressure of flying at high speed. They also wore a pilot's vest. The pockets held everything from a small penlight to a two-way radio. They also received their call signs. When pilots talk to the control tower, they identify themselves by their call signs. Wright's call sign was Basher Five-One. O'Grady's was Basher Five-Two.

The pilots took to the skies. Wright took the lead, about 2,000 feet (609 m) below O'Grady and a mile and a half (2.4 km) ahead. Their flight pattern was to make an oval pattern over the border between Croatia and Bosnia. The city of Bihac lay 5 miles (8 km) below. This was their "vul," or most vulnerable, time. It was when the pilots were in the greatest danger of being attacked.

They patrolled the area for about an hour, then ran low on fuel. They met up with a Boeing 707 plane, which served as a flying gas station. The 707 actually refueled their planes while they were flying!

1500 Hours (3:00 P.M.)

Although Wright and O'Grady didn't know it, a surface-to-air missile launcher was tracking them from the ground below. The launcher carried SA-6 missiles. These missiles could silently sail through the air at twice the speed of the F16s.

As Wright sped through the sky, his radar blipped. The system warned him that he'd been "spiked." That's when the enemy has spotted a pilot on its radar. Just as quickly, the blip disappeared. It could have been a false alarm.

1503 Hours (3:03 P.M.)

Suddenly, O'Grady was spiked by radar, too. Getting two false alarms seemed unlikely. The enemy could be waiting below, figuring out the

To keep their missions from being cut short, F-16 pilots were often instructed to refuel while they were flying.

plane's location. They could be preparing to launch an attack. Seconds later, O'Grady spotted a bright red flash just in front of his jet. Adrenaline pumped through his veins. It wasn't a false alarm. It was a missile. Someone was firing at the pilots. A second deadly missile would soon be on its way.

A split second later, Wright yelled into his radio, "Missiles in the air!"

An explosion thundered in the air. The second missile tore through the belly of O'Grady's jet. His F-16 split in two. The cockpit shook and rattled.

Jet fuel poured out and lit on fire. Flames danced through the cockpit, burning O'Grady's cheek and neck. O'Grady leaned forward and gripped the yellow triangular handle of his ejector. He pulled with all his might. The jet's canopy tore away. His seat flew into the sky, taking him with it.

O'Grady was 5 miles (8 km) above Earth. The oxygen level was very thin. O'Grady went into a short free fall. He then popped his parachute at 24,000 feet (732 m), praying it would open and slow his fall.

To his relief, it did. The parachute filled with air. O'Grady still had 4 miles (6.4 km) to fall before reaching the ground—a slow, dangerous drop. What if he was spotted before he reached the ground? Even if he did make it to Earth undetected, what waited for him below? Would the enemy make him a prisoner of war? Did Captain Wright even know O'Grady had survived

Although F-16s were keeping the peace in Bosnia, their missions were far from peaceful. Enemy weapons could strike at any time. Here, in 1995, Bosnian Serbs fire an anti-aircraft cannon into the skies.

the missile's impact? O'Grady switched on his radio beacon, or high-pitched alarm, for a few seconds. This sound would pinpoint his position. It would let the U.S. Air Force know he survived the blast. Of course, it would also alert the enemy that he was headed toward the ground. He had to risk it, though.

▲ Although O'Grady survived the attack over Bosnian skies, his jet was blown apart. This picture shows a missile from his F-16 that crashed into an area of trees.

Once on the ground, O'Grady would be far from safe. Wherever he landed, he would be at risk of capture—even death. O'Grady would find no "friendlies," or allies, in Bosnia—only enemies. Any or all of the warring ethnic groups could be hunting for him. In fact, the hunt might have already begun.

Still—his fellow soldiers would rescue him. He had to believe this.

Three

Behind Enemy Lines

Drifting over a highway, O'Grady saw a truck pull over to the side of the road. It looked like one used for military purposes. O'Grady continued his slow fall. Finally, he smacked against the ground. Not knowing if his enemies were already looking for him, he scrambled for cover. He found a good place to hide under some exposed tree roots. O'Grady was scared. Several people must have seen the missile tear his F-16 apart, he thought. Wouldn't it be just a matter of time before he was captured?

Suddenly, O'Grady heard footsteps. He froze in his hiding spot, as two men walked right past him. They were civilians, not soldiers. In enemy territory, however, anyone could turn him in or

◄ As O'Grady drifted in his parachute, his relief that he had survived turned to fear. He knew that the ground below was filled with armed Bosnian Serbs like the group pictured here.

shoot him. Two more locals walked by O'Grady's hideout minutes later. These civilians were holding guns. O'Grady stayed still, terrified that the next thing he would feel might be a rifle's hard metal muzzle.

Suddenly O'Grady heard a frightening sound—gunshots. First one, and then another bouncing off a rock. Had someone seen him? Were the Bosnian Serbs trying to flush him out of hiding? Even if he survived the daylight hours, what would the night hold? Would soldiers wearing night vision goggles soon be joining the hunt? O'Grady had no answers. He tried to stay calm, but the rifles rang out repeatedly.

As the hours passed, O'Grady saw fewer Bosnians. He risked radio contact. "Anyone, Basher Five-Two," he said, using his call sign. There was no response.

He kept still until dark. Hours without movement cut off the blood flow to his legs. Muscle

If O'Grady came into contact with enemy soldiers like the ones pictured here, he had no way of knowing what they would do to him.

cramps set in. At last, he felt safe enough to stretch. He checked his pilot's vest. The penlight, flares, compass, whistle, and medical kit were still there. The radio he kept in a plastic bag worked just fine.

Day Two (June 3)

Past midnight, O'Grady moved deeper into the forest to find a better hiding place. Every noise he made—breaking twigs, swishing branches—made him nervous. Finally, he found a group of trees.

He tucked in tight against their trunks and broke out his survival kit.

O'Grady wrapped his tarp around him. He pulled the camouflage netting over the tarp. As dawn turned the black sky to gray, O'Grady realized his hiding place was too exposed. He quickly found better shelter.

One thing the survival kit didn't have was food rations. O'Grady had never packed granola bars. Though hungry, he knew he could go without food for quite a while. Still, he longed for a bite of something. Survival training taught O'Grady how to test leaves to see if they were edible. He placed a leaf against his lips, first on the outside, then on the inside. He felt no burning or tingling. He placed a sample on his tongue. Next, he chewed and swallowed. The leaves weren't poisonous, but they weren't tasty, either. A few hours later, he heard the whir of helicopter blades overhead. The hunt was on again.

Day Three (June 4)

O'Grady traveled at night. He was concerned about his shrinking water supply. He had started out with eight water packs, about one quart. That was too little to keep O'Grady going for long. Adults need at least two quarts of water a day, even when at rest. O'Grady had already gone three days on less than a quart. He remembered his instructors telling him that dehydration could cause serious problems. If he went three days without water, his thinking would become less clear.

▶ A Pilot's Survival Kit

Some of the items found inside the kit are:

- eight packs of water
- an empty water pouch
- a dark ski cap, woolen socks
- green wool mittens
- a tarp (a heavy, waterproof covering)
- camouflage netting
- a foil space blanket
- a knife

O'Grady's problems kept piling up. After reaching higher ground, he tried again to signal from his radio. He hoped that the altitude would make his signal clearer. His hopes were dashed, though. No one responded to his signal.

Day Four (June 5)

O'Grady started his day in a poor hiding place. In it, he could be spotted easily. It also provided no escape route. He saw birds and a black squirrel come near him. Either would have made a welcome meal, but he didn't dare try to catch them. The risk of being spotted was far too great.

Soon after, he took a chance and made a move in the daylight. He needed to locate a better place to hide. Once he found a better spot, O'Grady napped. His sleep came in short spurts. He had to be alert even when nodding off. Although he couldn't stay alive on his own forever, being found by the wrong people could prove just as deadly.

He woke to the sound of the ground trembling around him. Had he been found? The answer relieved him. It was two cows, strolling along the path beside him. The cows stopped right beside his feet. He didn't dare move. He knew a cowherder must be nearby. Moments later, O'Grady's guess was confirmed. The herder began ringing a bell. At least the loud ringing would let him know if the herder was coming closer. Finally, the cows left the area. O'Grady had avoided another danger.

That night, one of O'Grady's prayers was answered. Rain fell in heavy sheets. Everything was soaked. The thirsty pilot opened his mouth to catch every drop he could. As he swallowed, the burn in his throat went away. Using a sponge from his kit, he mopped up every raindrop, squeezing them all into a plastic bag.

Day Five (June 6)

O'Grady's radio had two modes. One was for sending and receiving messages. The other was for emitting, or sending out, the beacon signal. O'Grady switched his radio to beacon mode. He left it on for a few seconds, then turned it off to wait. After a few minutes he switched it on to Guard mode. Guard was the radio's speaking and listening channel.

"Basher Five-Two, this is Flashman…hear me." The alarm had worked! A pilot searching for O'Grady had heard the beacon.

O'Grady nearly screamed his reply: "Flashman, this is Basher Five-Two." He repeated his reply. Flashman said nothing. It was obvious Flashman couldn't hear O'Grady's voice. However, he had heard the beacon. Although concerned that Flashman couldn't hear him, O'Grady's spirits were lifted. NATO now knew he was calling them. There was hope for a rescue.

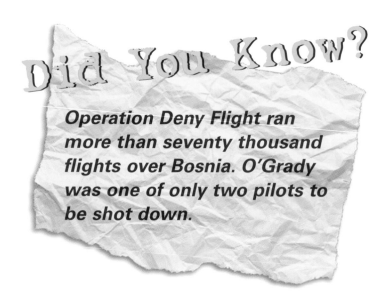

Did You Know?

Operation Deny Flight ran more than seventy thousand flights over Bosnia. O'Grady was one of only two pilots to be shot down.

Day Six (June 7)

Sometime during the day, O'Grady's next meal crawled over to him. A group of brown ants was eating a dead worm near his hand. Several of O'Grady's survival instructors had recommended eating ants. He never thought he'd agree to that menu item. Then again, he never thought he'd be this hungry. The ants of some countries are thought of as a sweet and popular treat. Bosnian ants, however, tasted like sour lemons. O'Grady wasn't about to be a food critic, though. He knew the ants would give him protein, vitamins, and minerals. He gladly gobbled over a dozen of them.

After his meal, Scott knew it was moving time again. He'd spent too much time in one spot. He found a small clearing and tried his radio again. He sat in the brutal cold, shivering, waiting for an answer. At 0206 hours (2:06 A.M.), he got one. He heard three clicks on the radio. Someone was reaching out to him!

When O'Grady stepped aboard the USS *Kearsarge*, he knew he was safe from harm, and that his brush with death had ended.

Four

Daring Rescue

"Basher Five-Two, this is Basher One-One on Alpha." It was the voice of Captain T. O. Hanford, a friend of O'Grady's. Hanford was flying his jet nearby. He had just finished flying a mission, and was trying to make radio contact with O'Grady. Meanwhile, Hanford's command post wanted him to return. His jet was dangerously low on fuel. Hanford demanded a few more minutes from the post. His friend and fellow pilot was in trouble, and he was going to keep trying. Hanford called again, hoping to hear O'Grady's answer.

"Basher One-One...Basher Five-Two."

Hanford's eyes widened. The voice was faint. Could it really be O'Grady? Hanford asked for the message to be repeated. When O'Grady responded a second time, Hanford's voice cracked with emotion. His tank was nearly empty, so Hanford had to refuel. He promised to call back as quickly as he could.

By Dawn's First Light

Hanford kept his word. He reassured O'Grady, "They're rounding up the boys right now. They're throwing everything they have at you." This was no exaggeration. The rescue operation was enormous. Super Stallion helicopters would pick up O'Grady. Two fully armed Cobra assault helicopters would help them. The air support of F/A-18 Marine Hornets was also on hand to assist.

As dawn broke, O'Grady heard the Hornets roar overhead. He clicked on his radio. The Hornets identified O'Grady's exact location from his radio signal. Moments later, the helicopters rose over the treeline. O'Grady popped a bright red flare. "Directly overhead," he yelled into the radio.

By 0648 hours (6:48 A.M.) on June 8, the helicopters had their valuable cargo—Scott O'Grady—aboard. The danger, though, was not yet over. Serbs had been alerted to the rescue

O'Grady's commander in chief, President Bill Clinton, was overjoyed and relieved to learn that the rescue mission had succeeded.

mission. They began firing at will. Rounds of ammunition ripped through the Stallion. Missiles were launched at the helicopter. A marine gunner fired back. The rescue team flew out of firing range. It was over—the mission was accomplished.

Once out of harm's way, O'Grady received a complete medical exam. He had suffered second-degree burns on his cheeks and neck. His feet were badly swollen. He was hungry, dehydrated, and exhausted. Then, at 0830 hours (8:30 A.M.), he had a phone call in the captain's cabin. He wondered whether it was his mother or father.

It wasn't either parent at all. It was O'Grady's commander in chief, President Bill Clinton. President Clinton told O'Grady that the entire country had been on edge, waiting for his rescue.

Welcome Home, Hero

Once Captain O'Grady was shipped back to the United States, he was flooded with warm welcomes. Of course, seeing his parents at Andrews Air Force Base, Maryland, was the greatest reunion of all. His father had lost 18 pounds worrying about his son. Scott himself had lost 25 pounds. On June 12, the O'Grady family joined President Clinton for lunch at the White House. Scott feasted on lamb chops and crabmeat. He told President Clinton he was going to pass on the salad. Clinton laughed. He knew that Scott had dined on enough leaves in Bosnia.

O'Grady has written two books about his close call with death. He's been the subject of countless interviews. This popularity surprised O'Grady. He only felt he was only doing his duty. He has described himself not as a hero but as a survivor.

- June 2, 1995—1315 hours (1:15 P.M.) Captain O'Grady takes off from Italy for a UN mission in Bosnia.
- 1503 hours (3:03 P.M.) O'Grady's F-16 is shot down by a Serbian missile.

Over the next six days, O'Grady survives behind enemy lines. He cannot approach soldiers or civilians. Anyone could be an enemy. They could turn him in as a hostage— or worse. O'Grady hides out during the day, and moves during the brutally cold nights. He uses his radio to send out distress signals, but receives no reply. He quickly runs out of water and becomes hungry. To nourish himself, O'Grady eats leaves and ants. He gathers falling rain in a sponge for water. He is almost spotted by men several times. Some of the men are carrying guns. Finally, O'Grady makes radio contact with a fellow pilot. The U.S. Air Force and Marines rescue O'Grady from Bosnia.

- June 8, 1995—0206 hours (2:06 A.M.) O'Grady makes radio contact with pilot Captain T. O. Hanford.
- 0648 hours (6:48 A.M.) O'Grady is picked up by marines during a daring daylight rescue.

adrenaline (uh-**dren**-uh-lin) a chemical produced by your body when you are excited, frightened, or angry

ammunition (am-yuh-**nish**-uhn) things that can be fired from weapons, such as bullets

camouflage (**kam**-uh-flazh) coloring or covering that makes animals, people, and objects look like their surroundings

canopy (**kan**-uh-pee) a shelter over something

civilians (si-**vil**-yuhnz) people who are not members of the armed forces

dehydration (dee-**hye**-dray-shun) a condition when you do not have enough water in your body

ejector (i-**jehkt**-ur) a special seat that hurls pilots out of a cockpit during an emergency

ethnic (**eth**-nik) to do with a group of people sharing the same national origins, language, or culture

exaggeration (eg-**zaj**-uh-ray-shun) making something seem bigger, better, and more important than it really is

NEW WORDS

facilities (fuh-**sil**-uh-tees) buildings that are used for a particular purpose

hostage (**hoss**-tij) someone taken and held prisoner as a way of demanding money or other conditions

muzzle (**muhz**-uhl) the open end of a gun barrel

rations (**rash**-uhnz) limited amounts of food

skeptical (**skep**-tuh-kuhl) when someone doubts that something is really true

sonic boom (**son**-ik **boom**) the loud noise produced by a jet when it travels faster than the speed of sound and breaks through the sound barrier

spiked (**spiked**) to be picked up on an enemy's radar

squadron (**skwahd**-ruhn) a group of ships, cavalry troops, or other military units

vulnerable (**vuhl**-nur-uh-buhl) being in a weak position and likely to be hurt in some way

FOR FURTHER READING

Holden, Henry M. *Air Force Aircraft*. Berkeley Heights, NJ: Enslow Publishers, Inc., 2001.

Langley, Wanda. *The Air Force in Action*. Berkeley Heights, NJ: Enslow Publishers, Inc., 2001.

O'Grady, Scott F., with Jeff Coplon. *Return With Honor*. New York: Doubleday, 1995.

O'Grady, Scott F., with Michael French. *Basher Five-Two*. New York: Bantam Doubleday Dell, 1997.

Sweetman, Bill. *Supersonic Fighters: The F-16 Fighting Falcons*. Minneapolis, MN: Capstone Press, 2001.

RESOURCES

Web Sites

The Rescue
www.allstar.fiu.edu/aero/ogrady.htm
Read a detailed description of the rescue of Scott O'Grady.

F-16 Fighting Falcon
www.fas.org/man/dod-101/sys/ac/f-16.htm
This site provides information, diagrams, and photos of the F-16 fighter jet.

O'Grady Interview
www.courttv.com/talk/chat_transcripts/2001/1015ogrady.html
View Court TV's personal interview with Captain Scott O'Grady.

RESOURCES

O'Grady's F-16 Found

www.usafe.af.mil/news/news00/uns00144.htm

This air force news release describes the recovery of O'Grady's jet five years after his F-16 was shot down.

Video

The Thunderbirds and the F-16

Director: Don Flagg. ASIN: 1586800434

Watch precision flying of F-16s from the best of the military flyers—the Thunderbirds. There are also pilot interviews and air-to-air footage.

INDEX

INDEX

ABOUT THE AUTHOR

Barbara A. Somervill is a freelance writer from South Carolina.